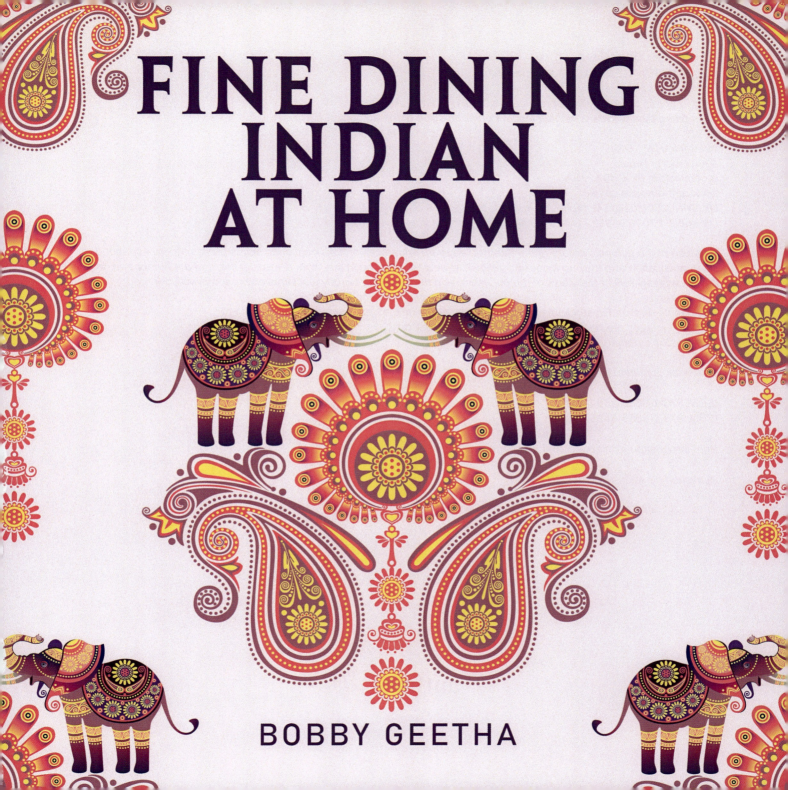

FINE DINING INDIAN AT HOME

BOBBY GEETHA

AuthorHouse™ UK
1663 Liberty Drive
Bloomington, IN 47403 USA
www.authorhouse.co.uk
UK TFN: 0800 0148641 (Toll Free inside the UK)
UK Local: 02036 956322 (+44 20 3695 6322 from outside the UK)

Because of the dynamic nature of the Internet, any web addresses or links contained in this book may have changed
since publication and may no longer be valid. The views expressed in this work are solely those of the author and do
not necessarily reflect the views of the publisher, and the publisher hereby disclaims any responsibility for them.

Any people depicted in stock imagery provided by Getty Images are models,
and such images are being used for illustrative purposes only.
Certain stock imagery © Getty Images.

This book is printed on acid-free paper.

ISBN: 978-1-6655-9604-6 (sc)
ISBN: 978-1-6655-9605-3 (e)

Print information available on the last page.

Published by AuthorHouse 03/11/2022

Contents

Non Vegetarian Main

Dessert

Beverage

Chef Bobby Geetha— An Introduction

Chef Bobby Geetha is a renowned name in the Indian culinary world and has contributed in deciphering and providing unique Indian dishes as well as unique cooking methods of Indian recipes.

Beyond the person in the elegant chef apron, Bobby Geetha is an incredible personality. His passion for cooking, creative food plating ideas, and excellent managerial and consultancy skills is what makes him a wonderful person. He is the highly rated finalist in BBC's *MasterChef: The Professionals season 8, Contenstant in BBC two Great British Menu series 17 Represnting North* and has also worked with renowned Michelin-starred culinary chefs. Chef Bobby Geetha has played a quintessential role in popularising Indian cuisines in the global culinary world wherein Indian cuisine is merely considered to be an 'old-fashioned curry' and 'spicy food'. He has sixteen years of managerial experience in five-star hotel kitchens and has specialisation in different food concepts ranging from fine dining to ghost kitchen outlets. Chef Bobby Geetha is known for creating bespoke packages which are based on the needs of the clients, ranging from staff training to menu design. The business is promoted through website, magazine, and social media channels.

According to Chef Bobby Geetha, food has always been an institution for him to explore more. This is evident from his recipes and cooking patterns, wherein he ensures to adapt classical and traditional recipes as per modern technique and taste. He is a dedicated professional who manages to modernise food yet still retain its authentic integrity. Chef Bobby Geetha takes immense pleasure in making Indian cuisine appeal to the international level.

YouTube Channel and Recipes—An Introduction

Tracing the rising popularity of Indian cuisine, Chef Bobby Geetha started his own YouTube channel to provide most amazing Indian food recipes. The main intent was to delve into more workable recipes and share them with the world. According to Chef Bobby Geetha, Indian food practices and cuisine have the answer to almost anything. It is because of this reason that his YouTube channel reinforces Indian cuisine as well as home kitchens, because it is essentially the need of the hour. Chef Bobby Geetha firmly believes that there are many hidden treasures in Indian cooking, and reconnecting with home food in a modern way is a good way to introduce the audience to Indian cuisine. The YouTube channel has a hand-picked collection of vegetarian and non-vegetarian dishes ranging from black butter chicken to crushed ginger spring onion chutney. There are a handful of chicken recipes which are cooked at a home kitchen following restaurant standards. Some of the recipes include easy steamed chicken, homemade butter chicken thigh finishing recipe, and whole fried chicken with Indian spices. These chicken video recipes provide content which engages the viewers and induces them to cook the same recipes in home kitchens. For instance, the recipe of black butter chicken is intriguing to watch because it engages the viewers to try this unique and simple recipe wherein activated charcoal is incorporated in the makhani sauce. Creative food plating acts as a cherry on the top. Likewise, the YouTube channel also provides a plethora of fish recipes such as fish in coconut meen molly, tandoori pomfret, masala fish fry, and many more. To further provide assistance to viewers, the channel has videos providing useful hacks and tips on how to clean and fry fish. In all, Bobby Geetha's YouTube channel provides a road map on how to make amazing fish recipes from the start.

One of the most striking features of this YouTube channel is the learning materials from the fine dining Indian magazine. There are many videos pertaining to chef consultancy, restaurant business, and Indian restaurants. For instance, there are videos on what can be learnt from Sanjeev Kapoor in the restaurant business, which helps audiences engage in career options in the culinary world and learn how the restaurant business can be started and grown. With regards to vegetarian dishes, many recipes are provided on the channel out of which most of them are basic recipes with a tinge of intricate fusion ideas, making recipes more drool-worthy. For instance, asparagus, celery and potato thoran are a nice fusion vegan dish which comes Southern India. The best part about such recipes and videos is that they tend to focus on regional cuisines of India and help portray Indian cuisine as a wide palette of varied taste in the global culinary world.

Snacks/Starter

Avocado Pakora

In Indian cuisine, spicy fritters are known as pakoras. Pakoras are made of vegetables which are coated with gram flour. Avocado pakoda is a fusion recipe including avocado in fritters.

Video: **https://www.youtube.com/watch?v=zvWP3FwjrC4&t=69s**

INGREDIENTS

3 tablespoons (45 grams) plain flour, plus extra 3 tbsp for dusting

1 tablespoon (15 grams) chickpea flour, also known as gram flour

1 Tablespoon (Approx 10 grams) rice flour

1/4 teaspoon (1 gram) turmeric powder

1/2 teaspoon (3 grams) chilli powder

1/4 teaspoon (2 grams) seasoning powder

1 pinch (1 gram) asafoetida

1 teaspoon (7 grams) chopped coriander leaves

1 teaspoon (7 grams) ginger-garlic paste

1/4 teaspoon (1 gram) baking powder

1/4 teaspoon (2 grams) salt

oil for deep frying

8 tablespoons (110 grams) water

1 avocado, not too over-ripe

2 tablespoons (30 grams) avocado chutney

1 pinch (1 gram) chat masala

METHOD

- Put all ingredients except avocado, avocado chutney, and chat masala in a mixing bowl. Add a small amount of water and mix to make a fine paste. Add the remaining water and mix until it forms a light thick batter. Set aside.
- Split open the avocado, take out the pit, and carefully scoop out the flesh from the skin. Reserve the avocado skin to present the pakora. Cut avocado flesh into wedges.
- Arrange the avocado wedges on a chopping board or plate. Dust with some chat masala and plain flour.
- Turn the sides and repeat the dusting process.
- Slowly dip the wedges into the batter and deep fry for 3 minutes at 170 degrees C.
- When crispy, remove and drain excess oil on a kitchen towel.

For plating

- Fill the avocado skin with avocado chutney and place the fried pakora wedges on top.
- Garnish and serve.

Beef Porotta

This recipe is an incredible combination and traditional dish of Sothern part of India, Kerala. Beef masala and porotta provides perfect amount of carbohydrates and protein. Here we are using water buffalo to make curry. In this video we take this amazing combination to a small plate concept.

Video: https://www.youtube.com/watch?v=_DpU-phq7rg

INGREDIENTS

For sauté porotta
1 teaspoon (7 grams) ghee

For beef masala

3 ladles beef curry with beef pieces
1/4 teaspoon (2 grams) fresh ginger, julienned
3 curry leaves
2 green chillies, sliced
1 tablespoon (15 grams) onion tomato masala

1 piece porotta, half cooked and shredded

1/2 teaspoon (4 grams) coriander powder
1/4 teaspoon (3 grams) garam masala
salt for seasoning
pickled ginger and onion for garnish

METHOD

To make sauté porotta

- In a pan, throw in the shredded porotta, add ghee, sauté and fry until it becomes little crispy.
- When it is done, take it out from the pan and keep it aside.

To make beef masala

- In the same pan, pour beef curry and add rest of the ingredients except salt and pickled ginger and onion.
- Sauté until the gravy thickens; check seasoning and add salt if needed.

For plating

- Put fried shredded porotta in the middle of the plate.
- Place beef masala on top of the porotta and garnish it with pickled ginger and onion.
- Serve it.

Charcoal Bubble Waffle Dosa

Dosa is a rice pancake from the southern part of India. It comes from a fermented batter made out of rice and urid dal. In this recipe, we are mixing an edible charcoal into the dosa batter to get a black colour. It is made in two ways, by using a bubble waffle maker and by having a traditional crepe-style dosa with some chilli and cheese.

Video: https://www.youtube.com/watch?v=Pw74JWGm_5E

INGREDIENTS

For the filling

1 tablespoon (30 grams) mature cheddar cheese
1 teaspoon (7 grams) green chillies, chopped

1 tablespoon (30 grams) onion, chopped
1/2 teaspoon (3 grams) coriander leaf, chopped

For charcoal dosa batter

3 ladles dosa batter, fermented
1 teaspoon (7 grams) charcoal powder

A pinch (1 gram) gunpowder

METHOD

- Put all the filling ingredients in a bowl. Mix together and set it aside.
- In a bowl, pour the dosa batter and add charcoal powder to it. Mix until it gets the exact black colour.

To make dosa in bubble waffle maker

- Apply clarified butter in bubble waffle maker.
- Pour the charcoal dosa batter evenly.
- Put the chilli and cheese mixture in each bubble pocket.
- Cover the chilli cheese mixture by drizzling dosa batter on top.
- Cover the bubble waffle maker and cook for 3 minutes.
- When it is cooked, open, slowly pick it up from waffle maker, and place it on a chopping board.

For plating

- Slightly chop the sides and cut it in half without cutting through the bubble.
- Place it in a bowl and sprinkle some gunpowder on top before serving.

To make dosa traditionally

- Apply some clarified butter on tawa. Pour charcoal dosa batter and spread it into a circle.
- Put in the chilli and cheese mixture and pour some ghee or oil on top.
- Ensure it is cooked evenly and is easy to remove from all sides.
- Slowly try to roll it and leave it on the pan to make it little more crispy.

For plating

- Plate it as shown in the video.

Chicken Vada Pav

Chicken vada pav is an Indian street food made by sandwiching a deep-fried chicken patty in pav or a bun with a generous amount of chutney. This is an Indian version of a chicken sandwich or burger.

Video: https://www.youtube.com/watch?v=q1sA1eHlUho

INGREDIENTS

For vada mix

3 teaspoons (20 grams) oil
A pinch (2 grams) asafoetida
½ teaspoon (3 grams) black mustard seeds
2 tablespoons (30 grams) chopped onion
2–3 curry leaves

A pinch (1 gram) turmeric powder
1/2 cup (120 grams) diced chicken
1/2 cup (100 grams) boiled potato
2 green chillies, sliced

For batter

2 tablespoons (30 grams) rice flour
5 tablespoons (70 grams) gram flour
1/4 teaspoon (2 grams) baking soda

1/4 teaspoon (2 grams) turmeric powder
1/4 teaspoon (2 grams) salt
4 tablespoons (50 grams) water

For frying

oil to deep fry
6 medium onion rings

fried boondhi, using the leftover batter
2 green chillies

For plating

2 mini brioche buns, cut in half
2 fried vada
sweet yoghurt, to drizzle

2 tablespoons (30 grams) fried boondhi
2 cheddar cheese slices
2 green chillies, fried

METHOD

To make vada mix

- In a pan, pour oil. When the oil is hot, add asafoetida.
- Add mustard seeds and allow them to crack.
- Add chopped onions and sauté for 2 minutes.
- Add curry leaf and turmeric powder and sauté for a minute.
- Add diced chicken and sauté until the chicken cooks.

- Add boiled potato and sliced green chilli.
- Sauté and slightly crush the boiled potato.
- The mix to make vada is ready. Make it into small vada balls of 60 grams and set aside.

To make batter

- In a mixing bowl, put all the ingredients mentioned in the batter mix.
- Mix all the ingredients and make it in to a thick paste.

For frying

- Slightly press the vada balls to make a flat patty.
- Dip the patty in to the batter and deep fry in oil at 180 degrees C for 5 minutes.
- Take out the fried patty and put it in on a towel to drain the excess oil.
- In the same batter, dip the onion rings and deep-fry them in the oil.
- Put the leftover batter in a squeeze bottle.
- Squeeze and allow the batter to drip into the hot oil to make boondhi.
- Set the fried boondhi on a towel.
- Fry the green chillies and set aside.

For plating

- Toast the brioche buns with butter.
- Place the butter-toasted brioche bun halves on a plate.
- Put chicken vada on each half of brioche bun.
- Drizzle sweet yoghurt on top of the vada.
- Place some fried boondhi on top of the vada.
- Put fried green chilli on top of the vada.
- Place sliced cheddar cheese on other two halves of the bun and combine with the vada buns to make sandwiches.
- Chicken vada pav is ready and served with fried onion rings.

Chicken Wings Desi Indo-Chinese Recipe

This is a fusion Indo-Chinese recipe made using buffalo chicken wings. This is an easy spicy chicken wing recipe and is delicious to serve with rice or any type of bread.

Video: https://www.youtube.com/watch?v=PrijMGCGt3U&t=28s

INGREDIENTS

2 tablespoons (30 grams) oil
1.5 kg (1500 grams) chicken wings
1/3 teaspoon (3 grams) black pepper powder
1/2 teaspoon (5 grams) salt, divided
1 chicken stock cube
1 teaspoon (7 grams) garlic, julienned
1 medium onion, chopped
1/2 teaspoon (4 grams) turmeric powder
1/2 teaspoon (4 grams) chilli powder

2 tablespoons (30 grams) tomato ketchup
3 tablespoons (45 grams) dark soya sauce
2 Holland red chillies, sliced
1/4 teaspoon (3 grams) chat masala
3 spring onion, sliced
4 coriander leaves, fresh
1/2 teaspoon (4 grams) black and white sesame seeds, toasted

METHOD

- In a thick-bottom pan. pour oil.
- When the oil is hot, place chicken wings into the oil.
- Add black pepper powder and 1/4 teaspoon of salt. Cook for 3 minutes.
- Turn the sides of the chicken wings and cook for another 3 minutes.
- Add chicken stock cubes, garlic, chopped onion, turmeric powder, chilli powder, and the remaining salt.

- Sauté for 2–3 minutes until the onions become translucent.
- Pour tomato ketchup, soya sauce, and Holland red chilli. Mix.
- To finish it off, add chat masala, spring onion, and coriander leaves. Mix and switch off the flame.

For plating

- Place the chicken wings in a bowl or on a plate and top with the veggies from the sauce.
- Sprinkle some black and white sesame seeds on top and serve.

Dosa Pizza

Dosa pizza is a south Indian style dosa pizza. It is made out of dosa batter and created like a pizza with cheese. It is more interesting than a normal pizza and is a healthier option considering it is gluten-free.

Video: https://www.youtube.com/watch?v=qt1znFDudic&t=1s

2 ladles dosa batter

1 tablespoons (15 grams) coconut chutney

1 tablespoons (15 grams) onion tomato masala

1 tablespoons (15 grams) mozzarella cheese

METHOD

- In a hot tawa, pour dosa batter, cover, and allow to cook for 1 minute.
- Turn the side and spread coconut chutney and onion tomato masala on top of dosa.
- Put mozzarella cheese on top.
- Cover and cook for 2 minutes on slow to medium heat until the cheese melts.
- Dosa pizza is ready and should be served hot.

Fried Egg Sandwich Pakora

This is a fried sandwich filled with potato and boiled egg. Fried bread or bread pakora is a famous street food breakfast that is very popular in Delhi. This recipe was developed when a Korean egg fried egg sandwich was combined with bread pakora.

Video: https://www.youtube.com/watch?v=keGGao6iUss&t=1s

For filling

1 large potato, boiled with turmeric
1 boiled egg, cut into cubes
1/4 teaspoon (2 grams) green chilli, chopped
4 coriander leaves

1 tablespoon (15 grams) mayonnaise
1 tablespoon (15 grams) tomato ketchup
1/2 cup (50 grams) mozzarella cheese, grated

To stuff bread

6 slices toasted bread

1 tablespoon (15 grams) mayonnaise

Batter for frying and sealing

2 teaspoons (14 grams) corn flour
4 teaspoons (28 grams) plain flour

1/2 cup water
oil, to deep-fry

Method

For filling

- In a mixing bowl, put all the ingredients mentioned in the filling.
- Mix and crush using a whisk.

To stuff bread

- Make a batter using corn flour, plain flour, and water and set it aside.
- Make a thick paste using corn flour, plain flour, and water.
- On toasted bread slice, remove crust and apply mayonnaise.
- Place potato egg filling on top of the bread and spread evenly to the edges.
- To seal the bread, take thick paste and apply on the sides. Slightly press to seal properly.
- Dip the bread into the thin batter and deep-fry it in the oil (170 degrees C).
- Cook both sides 2 minutes each until it turns to nice golden-brown colour.
- After frying, keep it on a towel to drain the excess oil.
- Cut it into two halves and serve it hot, ideally with a mint chutney.

Mince Beef and Black Pudding Sausage Roll

This is a new and different recipe which uses minced beef and black pudding, which is a black sausage consisting of pork, suet, and dried pig's blood.

Video: https://www.youtube.com/watch?v=XRso1eB1CeY&t=34s

For filling

2 cups (300 grams) minced beef
1 cup (200 grams) black pudding
1/2 cup (100 grams) chopped onion
1/2 cup (100 grams) chopped potato, boiled
3/4 teaspoon (5 grams) seasoning liquid
1/4 teaspoon (2 grams) green chilli, chopped

1 teaspoon (7 grams) chilli powder
1/2 teaspoon (3 grams) turmeric powder
1 tablespoon (15 grams) coriander powder
1 tablespoon (15 grams) stock cube
1/2 teaspoon (3 grams) salt

For roll

1 puff pastry sheet
1 egg yolk
1 tablespoon (15 grams) water

1 teaspoon (7 grams) fennel seeds
1 teaspoon (7 grams) black and white sesame seeds

For plating

1 tablespoon (15 grams) tadka mayonnaise pickled onions and ginger

1/4 teaspoon (1 gram) Holland red chilli, sliced

METHOD:

For filling

- In a mixing bowl, put the minced beef and all the ingredients in the filling section except black pudding. Mix well.
- Add the black pudding to the mixture and mix it without breaking the black pudding.
- The best way to dice the black pudding is to semi-freeze it before cutting into cubes.

For roll

- In a cling film, put the mixture, roll it tightly, and make a nice cylindrical shape so it fits inside the puff pastry.
- Place sausage in the fridge to get set.

- To make the egg wash, break the egg, separate the egg yolk, and keep the egg yolk in a bowl.
- Add a pinch of turmeric powder and water into the yolk and beat it.
- Apply the egg wash on the puff pastry sheet. Place the sausage and roll the sheet over the sausage.
- Cut the excess sheet off and place it in a baking tray.
- Using your fingers, press and close the open ends.
- Using a fork, press the edges and apply egg wash on top the sausage roll. This gives it a nice colour.
- With a sharp knife, lightly cut the top of the sausage roll so the steam escapes. It also gives it a nice crust.
- Sprinkle some fennel seeds and black and white sesame seeds on top of the roll.
- Place it in the oven and cook it for 25 minutes at 170 degrees C.

For plating

- Using a nice bread knife, cut the sausage roll and place it on a plate.
- Spoon tadka mayonnaise on the plate.
- Garnish with pickled onions and ginger and Holland red chilli.

Onion Bhaji Recipe with Leeks and Savoy Cabbage

This recipe is an amazing makeover of onion bhaji. Here, we are using leek, savoy cabbage, onion, and potatoes to make bhaji with all English vegetables. Bhaji is a hot, spicy snack similar to a fritter and originated in India.

Video: https://www.youtube.com/watch?v=6zL7FoTPLtY&t=1s

INGREDIENTS

1/2 savoy cabbage (leaves only), shredded
1 medium onion, sliced
1 leek stem
1 small potato, sliced
2 green chillies
1 teaspoon (7 grams) crushed fennel
1 tablespoon (15 grams) ginger garlic paste

1 teaspoon (7 grams) turmeric powder
1/4 teaspoon (3 grams) asafoetida (hing)
1 teaspoon (7 grams) salt
4 tablespoons (60 grams) gram flour
1 tablespoon (15 grams) rice flour
oil, to fry

For garnish

2 tablespoons (30 grams) leek, sliced
1/4 teaspoon (3 grams) chat masala

1/4 teaspoon (3 grams) tamarind chutney

METHOD

- In a bowl, put the shredded savoy cabbage, sliced onions, sliced potatoes, sliced leeks, green chilli, and crushed fennel.
- Add ginger garlic paste, turmeric powder, asafoetida, and salt.
- Mix and set it aside for 30 minutes so the water comes out from the cabbage.
- Add gram flour and rice flour and mix well. The vegetable mixture for bhaji is ready.
- Make small balls of vegetable mixture without pressing it tight.
- In a frying pan, pour oil. When the oil is hot, drop the vegetable balls into the oil.
- Fry at 170 degrees C for 6 minutes.
- When it is ready, take it out from the oil and keep it on a kitchen towel to drain the excess oil.

For plating

- In a snack bowl, place butter paper and put the pakoras/bhaji.

For garnish

- Put some sliced leeks into the hot oil after switching off the fire.
- Fry it and set it aside.
- Sprinkle chat masala on top of the bhaji. Pour some tamarind chutney and fried leeks on top.
- Add some Holland red chilli for an extra kick.

Salmon Kebab Mini Skewer

This is an amazing restaurant-style salmon kebab skewer. It is an easy recipe and is so simple to make. These skewers are moist, flaky, and full of flavours, and they are perfect for cooking anytime.

Video: https://www.youtube.com/watch?v=4N0I3bNQfvw

INGREDIENTS

4 salmon filets, cut in 3 centimetre cubes
1 teaspoon (7 grams) ginger garlic paste
1 teaspoon (7 grams) mustard oil
1/4 teaspoon (3 grams) turmeric powder
1/4 teaspoon (3 grams) green chilli, chopped
1/2 teaspoon (4 grams) salt
1 teaspoon (7 grams) Orange juice

1/4 teaspoon (2 grams) ginger, chopped
1 teaspoon (7 grams) coconut milk powder
2 red bell peppers, cubed
2 green bell peppers, cubed
2 lemongrass skewers
oil, to pan-fry
1/2 teaspoon (5 grams) butter

For plating

1 teaspoon (7 grams) tadka mayonnaise
1 teaspoon (7 grams) corn salad

1 teaspoon (7 grams) bell pepper, julienned
A pinch (2 grams) chat masala

METHOD

- Marinate the salmon cubes for 30 mins with ginger garlic paste, mustard oil, turmeric powder, chopped green chilli, salt, orange juice, chopped ginger, and coconut milk powder. Mix well.
- Put the red and green bell pepper cubes into the marinade and mix well.
- Skewer and arrange the bell pepper cubes and salmon cubes on the lemongrass skewers.
- In a hot pan, pour some oil and put in the salmon skewer. Pan-fry it on a medium flame.
- Put butter on top of the salmon skewer to give extra flavour.
- Cook each side for 1 minute.
- When it is cooked evenly, take it out from the frying pan and plate it.

For plating

- on a serving plate, put some tadka mayonnaise. Place the salmon skewers on top of the mayonnaise.
- Put corn salad on top of the salmon skewer and garnish it with some julienned bell pepper.
- Sprinkle some chat masala on top and serve.

Spicy Chilli Walnuts

This is a great recipe with roasted chickpea and fried spicy chilli walnut. Walnuts are also called brain nuts. Walnuts are such a heart healthy ingredient and have as twice as many antioxidants as other nuts. You can use any kind of nut to adapt the recipe.

Video: https://www.youtube.com/watch?v=macCNRB_wXM

1/2 kg (500 grams) walnut
6 tablespoons (100 grams) oil
8–10 curry leaves
2 green chillies, slit

3 tablespoons (50 grams) roasted chickpea
1 tablespoons (15 grams) chilli powder
3/4 tablespoon (5 grams) salt

METHOD

- In a hot pan, pour oil. When the oil is hot, add walnuts.
- Fry walnuts until they turn a golden brown colour. Set aside in a bowl.
- In the same pan, using the leftover oil, add curry leaves, green chilli, and roasted chickpeas.
- Sauté until the chickpeas get crispy.
- Put the chickpeas and walnuts into a bowl.
- Add chilli powder and salt, toss, and serve.

Tapioca Poppadom

This is a fresh, home-made tapioca poppadom. A poppadom is a thin, crisp, round, flat bread from India. Poppadoms are made with black gram flour, but they can also be made from flour made from rice, chickpeas, and lentils.

Video: https://www.youtube.com/watch?v=UmU6jOeJtYY&t=225s

For poppadom

1 cup (250 grams) sago (tapioca granules)
3 cups (750 grams) water
1/4 teaspoon (2 grams) cumin seeds

salt, for seasoning
oil, to deep-fry

For onion tomato masala

1 tablespoon (15 grams) onion, chopped
1 tablespoon (15 grams) tomato, chopped
1 green chilli, chopped

1 tablespoon (15 grams) fresh coriander, chopped
1/4 teaspoon (3 grams) chat masala

METHOD

For making poppadom

- Put all the ingredients except oil in a thick-bottom pan and mix well.
- Cook it on a low flame until it foams and has a jelly-like texture.
- While cooking, continuously and gently mix with spatula.
- When cooking is done, spread it on a butter paper using a spatula.
- While spreading, keep medium thickness; do not go too thin or too thick.
- To dry, put in the oven at a temperature of 60 degrees C overnight.
- In a hot pan, pour oil to deep-fry. Oil should be really hot (above 200 degrees C).
- Put poppadom one by one into the oil and fry.
- Set aside on a kitchen towel to drain excess oil.

For making onion tomato masala

- Put all the ingredients mentioned in the onion tomato masala in a bowl and mix together.

For plating

- Place poppadom on a chopping board and spread the onion tomato masala on top the poppadom.
- Serve it as a teatime snack or as a starter before main meal.

Vegeterian Main

Aloo Gobi Masala

This is an amazing and easy recipe from India. Aloo gobi is a side dish made with potatoes, cauliflower, and Indian spices and is one of the simplest and tastiest side dish in Indian cuisine.

Video: **https://www.youtube.com/watch?v=tKsbFUhmO1I&t=40s**

For frying vegetables
2 medium potatoes(about 500 grams), boiled and cut into cubes

For masala

2 tablespoons (30 grams) oil
1/4 teaspoon (3 grams) asafoetida (*hing*)
1/2 teaspoon (4 grams) cumin seeds
1 teaspoon (7 grams) fresh ginger, julienned
1 medium onion, chopped
3 dried red chillies
1 tablespoon (15 grams) ginger-garlic paste
1/4 teaspoon (3 grams) turmeric powder
1/4 teaspoon (3 grams) chilli powder

For plating

1 chapatti
3 leaves coriander leaf for garnish

500 grams cauliflower
oil for frying

1 1/2 teaspoon (10 grams) coriander powder
2 medium tomatoes, chopped
1/2 vegetable stock cube
1 cup hot water
salt to taste
1/4 teaspoon (3 grams) chat masala
1 large mild green chilli
4 springs fresh coriander leaf

1 tablespoon (15 grams) yoghurt (omit or use a substitute for a vegan dish)

METHOD

Frying vegetables

- Pour oil into a thick-bottomed wok.
- When the oil is hot (170 degrees C), fry cauliflower for 5 minutes, then drain and set aside.
- Fry boiled potatoes for 5 minutes, drain, and set aside.

To make masala

- Heat oil for masala in the same wok.
- When the oil is hot, add asafoetida (hing), cumin seeds, half the julienned ginger, and onion.
- Sauté till onion is golden brown.

- Add dry red chilli and ginger-garlic paste. Sauté for 1 minute.
- Add turmeric powder, chilli powder, and coriander powder. Toss together and sauté for another minute.
- Add chopped tomatoes. Sauté for 2 minutes.
- Dissolve the vegetable stock cube in a cup of water.
- Add salt and cook for one more minute.
- To finish the masala, add chat masala, large green chilli, and the remaining fresh ginger julienne. Sauté for a minute.
- Return fried potatoes and cauliflower to wok and toss to mix with the masala.
- Tear the fresh coriander sprigs into pieces and stir into the masala.

For plating

- Place cooked and reheated chapatti on a round plate.
- Pour aloo gobi masala on top of the chapatti.
- Garnish with fresh coriander leaves and yoghurt (omit yoghurt for a vegan dish) as shown.

Asparagus, Celery, and Potato Thoran

This fantastic thoran comes from southern part of India and is a great side dish that goes well with rice. In this thoran, we are using British seasonal veggies which are locally produced, such as asparagus, celery, and potato. Thoran is a dish made with finely chopped vegetables cooked with shallots, spices, and freshly grated coconut.

Video: **https://www.youtube.com/watch?v=ga5rKuuLPSI&t=7s**

INGREDIENTS

2 green chillies
3 cloves garlic
1/2 teaspoon (4 grams) cumin seeds
1 tablespoon (15 grams) coconut oil
1/2 teaspoon (4 grams) mustard seeds
3 dried red chillies, whole
1 small onion (50 grams), chopped to yield about 3 tablespoons
1 medium potato, skin on and cut into 1-inch cubes
3/4 teaspoon (5 grams) salt

1/4 teaspoon (3 grams) turmeric powder
1/4 teaspoon (3 grams) black pepper powder
1 ladle (30 millilitres) water
1 cup (200 grams) asparagus, cut into 1-inch pieces
2 sticks celery, peeled and cut into thin slices
3 teaspoons (21 grams) fresh grated coconut
1 Holland red chilli, sliced (optional for hotter spice level)

METHOD

- Put garlic, green chilli, and cumin seeds in a mortar and pestle. Crush using the pestle and set aside.
- Pour coconut oil into a thick-bottomed pan. When the oil is hot, add mustard seeds and allow them to crack.
- Add dry red chillies and chopped onion. Sauté for about 1 minute.
- Add potato and sprinkle with salt, turmeric powder, and pepper powder. Sauté for 1 minute.
- Pour water over potato mixture, cover with a lid, and allow potato to cook over a slow flame for 5 minutes.
- When potato is cooked and tender, add asparagus and celery. Toss together and then cook 2–3 minutes.
- To finish off, add previously crushed garlic, green chilli, and cumin seeds. Sauté for 2 minutes and then add the freshly grated coconut. Add sliced Holland red chilli if you prefer an extra spicy dish.
- Serve in bowl as pictured.

Brussels Sprout Courgette Kalonji Masala

Brussel sprout courgette kalonji masala is a vegan Indian side dish which is often eaten with bread and rice. It is a healthy vegan subzi recipe with English vegetables. It can be in either dry or semi dry or gravy form.

Video: https://www.youtube.com/watch?v=NprIHrFb6j0&t=1s

This is a wonderful vegan subzi recipe with English vegetables. Subzi is a side dish which can be dry, semi-dry, or served with some gravy. This goes well with rice dish and with any type of bread.

INGREDIENTS

10 brussels sprouts
1 courgette, quartered length-wise
2 tablespoons (30 grams) oil
1/2 teaspoon (4 grams) kalonji (onion seed)
1 teaspoon (7 grams) garlic, julienned
1 teaspoon (7 grams) ginger
3 ladles onion tomato masala
½ teaspoon (3 grams) turmeric powder
1 teaspoon (7 grams) coriander powder

1 teaspoon (7 grams) chilli powder
6 baby plum tomatoes, cut in half
To finish
1 teaspoon (7 grams) ginger
4 coriander leaves
2 green chillies, sliced
1 teaspoon (7 grams) chat masala
salt, to taste

METHOD

- Blanch brussels sprouts in boiling water. Take out and put in ice-cold water to stop cooking. Doing this helps the vegetable cook and also gives it a nice colour.
- Do the same process for the courgettes.
- In a thick bottom pan, pour oil.
- When the oil is hot, put kalonji into the oil.
- Add ginger and garlic and sauté for a minute.
- Add 2 ladles of onion tomato masala, sauté, and cook for 2 minutes.
- Add turmeric powder, coriander powder, chilli powder, and baby plum tomatoes. Sauté.
- Throw in the blanched brussels sprouts and courgettes. Mix it all together.
- To finish it off, add one more ladle of onion tomato masala, some ginger, coriander leaves, and sliced green chilli. Mix well.
- Add chat masala. Check seasoning and add salt if needed.

For plating

- Serve in a portion bowl.

Makhani Sauce

Makhani sauce is also known as butter chicken sauce. It is a rich, creamy, and buttery tomato based sauce used to make many varieties of subzi. Makhani means something that has butter.

Video: https://www.youtube.com/watch?v=DoWGDxb3ocM&t=1s

For first base of makhani sauce

1.2 kg (1200 grams) chopped tomato (canned)
1 medium onion, sliced
6 garlic cloves, crushed
2 tablespoons (30 grams) ginger

1/2 teaspoon (4 grams) cardamom powder
1/4 teaspoon (3 grams) cloves, whole
1/2 teaspoon (3 grams) black pepper corns
1 litre hot water

For finishing stage of the sauce

1 teaspoon (7 grams) chilli powder
1 block (250 grams) butter
12 teaspoons (84 grams) sugar

1/2 teaspoon (4 grams) salt
10 tablespoons (150 grams) double cream

METHOD

For first base of makhani sauce

- In a thick-bottom pot, put all the ingredients mentioned in first base and allow it to boil.
- When it starts boiling, simmer it on a very low flame. Allow to cook for at least an hour.
- After an hour, switch off the flame and set it aside to rest.
- Let it cool down to lukewarm temperature and grind it into a fine, smooth paste.

For finishing stage of the sauce

- Keep the sauce on the flame and give it a boil.
- Add all the ingredients mentioned in finishing stage of sauce.
- Mix it all together and allow to cook for at least half an hour on a low flame.
- Switch off the flame. The makhani sauce is ready.

Pilaf Rice

Pilaf is a one pot rice dish cooking in water with adding some spices. Basmati rice is the best for both flavour and fluffiness. Basmati is a type of long grain rice, the longer the grain the fluffier the rice. It also has a lovely subtle fragrance.

Video: https://www.youtube.com/watch?v=2jofI5sbIUE&t=7s

1 kg (1000 grams) basmati rice (sella), soaked in water for 30 minutes and drained
1 ladle (30 grams) ghee
2 tablespoons (30 grams) whole spice
4 tablespoons (60 grams) sliced onions
1 teaspoon (7 grams) powdered cardamom

1 teaspoon (7 grams) powdered mace
1 medium lemon, with juice separated
1 teaspoon (7 grams) salt
1.7 litre (1700 grams) boiling water
4 mint leaves
1/4 teaspoon (2 grams) saffron strands

METHOD

- In a thick-bottom pot, pour ghee. When ghee is hot, add whole spices and sliced onions.
- Sauté for 3 minutes until the onion is slightly brown in colour.
- Add rice to the pot. Add powdered cardamom and powdered mace. Mix well.
- Pour in lemon juice and put lemon in to the rice.
- Add salt and pour water (for 1 kg rice, the water should be exact 1.7 litres).
- Bring to a boil so water gets absorbed.
- When water is absorbed, break the mint leaf with your hands and put it into the rice.
- Put saffron strands on top of the rice.
- Cover the pot with a tight lid and cook for 6 minutes on a slow flame.
- Switch off the fire and leave it for another 6 minutes.
- Open the lid and check whether the rice is cooked well.
- Pilaf is ready to serve.

Quail Egg Masala Crispy Dosa

This crispy masala dosa has an eggy twist as it makes use of Quail egg which is a delicacy. This dosa is a crispy thin wafer dosa and the quail egg masala adds flavour to it.

VIDEO LINK : https://www.youtube.com/watch?v=-ZtI-HjPMp4&t=3s

For Crispy dosa batter:

2 ladles (60 grams) dosa batter
2 ladles (60 grams) water

1 tablespoon (15 grams) oil

For quail egg masala

4 quail eggs, soft boiled
1 tablespoon (15 grams) oil
1/6 teaspoon (1 gram) ginger, julienned
2 tablespoons (30 grams) chopped onions
1 green chilli
1 teaspoon (7 grams) turmeric powder
1/2 teaspoon (3 grams) garam masala

1/4 teaspoon (1 gram) black pepper, crushed
1 tablespoon (15 grams) onion tomato masala
1/4 teaspoon (1 gram) chat masala
chopped coriander leaf (optional)
1/4 teaspoon (1 gram) salt
1 tablespoon (15 grams) water

For soft-boiled quail egg

boiling water

2 tablespoons (30 mL) vinegar

METHOD

For crispy dosa batter

- In mixing bowl, put dosa batter, water, and oil. Mix well using whisk and set it aside.

For soft-boiled quail eggs

- In a pan, boil water, put in quail eggs, and cook for 2 minutes.
- Take out the quail eggs. Put in a glass of ice-cold water mixed with vinegar for half an hour.
- This helps to reduce the strength of the eggshell, and it will be easy to peel off.

For quail egg masala

- In a hot pan, pour oil. Add all the ingredients mentioned in the quail egg masala and sauté for 5 minutes.
- If needed, you can add coriander leaf at the end.

To make crispy dosa

- In a hot pan, pour 2 ladles of batter. Allow it to spread it completely to a very thin layer.
- Make sure it gets a nice golden colour and cooks evenly.
- When it cooks, you can see it will be crispy and have a nice, web-like texture.
- Take the crispy dosa out from the pan and place it in a kitchen towel to drain the excess oil.
- Plate as shown in the picture.

Red Cabbage Thoran or Subzi

This fantastic cabbage thoran comes from the southern part of India and is a great side dish. It goes well with rice. Usually in South India, this thoran is made out of white cabbage tossed with coconut and a few spices such as cumin and mustard seeds. In this recipe, we are using red cabbage, and we make it into a completely different dish that gives a different flavour and aroma.

Video: https://www.youtube.com/watch?v=w6ZtV3t6NL8&t=6s

INGREDIENTS

2 tablespoons (30 grams) oil
½ teaspoon (3 grams) cumin seeds
½ teaspoon (3 grams) red chilli flakes
1 teaspoon (7 grams) roasted chickpeas
2 tablespoons (30 grams) onion, chopped
1 teaspoon (7 grams) chilli powder
1/4 teaspoon (2 grams) garam masala
2 green chillies, split

1/4 teaspoon (4 grams) turmeric powder
1 cup (250 grams) red cabbage, grated
1 tablespoon (15 grams) vinegar
3 tablespoons (45 grams) water
3 tablespoons (45 grams) onion tomato masala
1/4 teaspoon (3 grams) chat masala
2 coriander leaves
1 teaspoon (7 grams) salt

METHOD

- In a hot pan, pour oil. When the oil is hot, put in cumin seeds and allow them to crack.
- Put in red chilli flakes. Make sure not to burn the chilli flakes.
- Put in roasted chickpea and sauté for a minute.
- Now add chopped onion, green chilli, turmeric powder, chilli powder and garam masala.
- Sauté for two minutes, add grated red cabbage and salt. Mix well.
- Cover and cook for 5 minutes on a low flame.
- Pour vinegar into the cabbage to enhance colour and sour taste.
- Add water, turn flame to medium, cover, and allow to cook for 5 more minutes.
- Cabbage should be soft, but you should feel a light crunch while chewing.
- Add onion tomato masala and mix well.
- For finishing touch, add chat masala. Break coriander leaves and sprinkle on top. Mix.
- Check seasoning. Subzi is ready to serve.

Saag Aloo

Saag aloo is an amazing spiced dish made with potatoes and spinach. It makes a great side dish and can be served with a bowl of daal and some chappatis or rice.

Videos

Saag Aloo: https://www.youtube.com/watch?v=0Xbz0B40jng
Onion Tomato Masala: https://www.youtube.com/watch?v=Yvdb6eMVosI&t=1s

INGREDIENTS

9 baby potatoes, boiled
1 tablespoon (15 grams) olive oil
1/4 teaspoon (3 grams) mustard seeds
2 dry red chillies
1 teaspoon (7 grams) chopped garlic
1 tablespoon (15 grams) onion tomato masala

1/4 teaspoon (3 grams) turmeric powder
1/4 teaspoon (3 grams) salt
1 Holland red chilli, sliced
4 coriander sprigs, fresh
1/2 cup (100 grams) baby spinach
1 tablespoon (15 grams) lemon juice

METHOD

- Boil baby potatoes to 90% done.
- In an open grilling pan, grill the potatoes until they are nicely crispy and brown outside. Set aside.
- In a kadai, pour oil. When the oil is hot, add mustard seeds and allow them to crack.
- Add dry red chilli and chopped garlic. Sauté for a minute.
- Add onion tomato masala and sauté for another minute.
- Add turmeric powder and grilled baby potatoes.
- Mix and slightly crush the baby potatoes to bite-size pieces.
- Add salt and mix it.
- Add Holland red chilli and coriander leaf. Sauté and mix.
- Add the baby spinach and sauté for 2 minutes, leaving the slight crunchiness and green colour of the spinach.
- Finish the dish by adding lemon juice.
- Serve it hot in a nice white bowl.

String Hopper Upma

This is a delicious upma made from leftover string hoppers. Upma is a South Indian breakfast dish usually made with roasted sooji. This dish is made using one pan and gives an additional touch to string hopper upma by adding fried quail egg and onion tomato masala.

Video: https://www.youtube.com/watch?v=6UpxFgjjkjo&t=6s

INGREDIENTS

1 tablespoon (15 grams) oil
1/2 teaspoon (4 grams) mustard seeds
1/2 teaspoon (4 grams) roasted chickpeas
1 teaspoon (7 grams) ginger, julienned
1 tablespoon (15 grams) onion, chopped
1 green chilli, chopped
3 curry leaves
1/4 teaspoon (2 grams) turmeric powder

1 cup (250 grams) string hopper
2 tablespoons (30 grams) water
1/4 teaspoon (3 grams) salt
3 teaspoons (21 grams) onion tomato masala
3 quail eggs
1 tablespoon (15 grams) chilli-fried walnuts
1 teaspoon (7 grams) pickled onion and ginger

METHOD

- In a hot pan, pour the oil. When the oil is hot, put in mustard seeds and allow them to crack.
- Add roasted chickpeas, ginger, chopped onions, green chilli, and curry leaves.
- Sauté for 1 minute, add turmeric powder, and sauté for another minute.
- Add string hopper and mix slowly
- Pour some water to get a moist texture.
- Add salt and gently mix over a medium flame.
- Make 3 small holes through the upma. Spoon the onion tomato masala into the hole.
- Make a small hole through the onion tomato masala.

- Crack the quail egg and pour into the hole.
- Allow quail egg to cook at a very low heat. Make sure not to burn the upma.
- Once the quail egg is done, put some chilli-fried walnuts on top of the upma.
- Garnish with pickled onion and ginger and serve.

Trivandrum Kappa

This is a simple, easy, home-made tapioca (cassava) recipe from the southern part of India, in Kerala. Tapioca is called Kappa in the regional language Malayalam. Tapioca is widely consumed across Kerala. It is taken as breakfast or as a staple food. Mashed tapioca goes well with meat or fish curry, especially sardines, as a delicacy in Kerala.

Video: https://www.youtube.com/watch?v=pOvrIPoYQoM&t=61s

INGREDIENTS

2 tablespoons (30 grams) onion, chopped
4 garlic cloves
3 green chillies
1/2 teaspoon (4 grams) cumin seeds
6 curry leaves

1 tablespoon (15 grams) coconut oil
1 kg (1000 grams) tapioca
2 litres water
1 teaspoon (7 grams) turmeric powder
1 teaspoon (7 grams) salt

METHOD

- Using a mortar and pestle, crush onion, garlic, green chilli, cumin seeds, and curry leaf together.
- Add coconut oil to it. Crush and mix it altogether. Set it aside.
- Wash and clean tapioca and put it in a thick-bottom pot.
- Pour water into it. Add turmeric powder and salt.
- Allow to boil and cook until the tapioca is soft.
- Drain out the boiled water, leaving some water in the pot.
- Add the crushed mixture to tapioca and mix well.
- Using a wooden spatula, gently mash tapioca by leaving some bite-size pieces.
- Serve it in a bowl.

Walnut and Pumpkin Kadi

Kadi is a light, spicy vegetarian gravy dish made out of besan flour (gram flour) and sour yoghurt. It is mostly made in northern parts of India. In southern parts of India, this is prepared in different way without besan flour; instead, they use ground grated coconut with some cumin and green chilli. Kadi goes well with rice.

VIDEO LINK : https://www.youtube.com/watch?v=KyJ49YTfvdA&t=2s

1 cup (250 grams) pumpkin, peeled and cut into cubes
2 tablespoons (30 grams) oil
1/4 teaspoon (2 grams) asafoetida
1/2 teaspoon (4 grams) mustard seeds

2 tablespoons (30 grams) chopped onion
1/2 teaspoon (4 grams) salt
1/4 teaspoon (3 grams) turmeric powder
2 tablespoons (30 grams) walnuts
2 coriander leaves

Yoghurt mix for the kadi

1 cup (250 grams) yoghurt
1 tablespoon (15 grams) gram flour
1/4 teaspoon (3 grams) red chilli flakes
1/2 teaspoon (4 grams) turmeric powder
1/4 teaspoon (3 grams) chilli powder

1/4 teaspoon (3 grams) black pepper powder
1/4 teaspoon (3 grams) salt
A pinch (2 grams) garam masala
1 cup water

To pan-fry pumpkin wedges (for plating)

3 pumpkin wedges, peeled
1/2 teaspoon (5 grams) ginger garlic paste
1/4 teaspoon (3 grams) turmeric powder

1/2 teaspoon (5 grams) chilli powder
Oil, to pan-fry

Garnish

3 coriander leaves
chilli oil, to drizzle

coriander oil, to drizzle

METHOD

Yoghurt mix for kadi

- In a mixing bowl, put all the ingredients mentioned in the yoghurt mix for kadi.
- Using a whisk, mix all the ingredients. Make sure there are no lumps.
- When it is ready, set it aside.

To make pumpkin kadi

- In a hot pan, pour oil. When the oil is hot, put in asafoetida and mustard seeds. Allow mustard seeds to crack.
- Add chopped onions and sauté for a 3 minutes.
- Pu pumpkin cubes into the pan. Add salt and sauté for 2 minutes.
- Add turmeric powder and sauté for 1 minute. Then cover and cook until the pumpkin is soft.
- Add in walnuts and sauté for another 1 minute.
- Pour the yoghurt mix into the pan and mix gently. Bring it to a boil on medium heat.
- The pumpkin kadi is ready. Break fresh coriander by hand and throw it into the kadi.

To pan-fry pumpkin wedges

- Marinate for 5 mins the pumpkin wedges with ginger garlic paste, turmeric powder, and chilli powder.
- In a hot pan, pour oil. When the oil is hot, place the pumpkin wedges into the oil.
- Cover and cook on medium heat until they get a nice golden brown colour.
- Turn the side, cover, and cook for 1 minute.
- When it is ready, take it out from the pan and set it aside for plating.

For plating

- In a serving bowl, pour pumpkin kadi with pumpkin pieces and walnuts from the kadi.
- Place the pan-fried pumpkin wedges on top of the kadi.
- Garnish with coriander leaf. Drizzle some chilli oil and coriander oil.

Non Vegetarian Main

Beef Curry Kappa

This recipe is an amazing combination of tapioca and beef curry. It is a traditional recipe of Kerala, in the southern part of India, that goes well with rice, chapatti, or any type of bread.

Video: **https://www.youtube.com/watch?v=dQcaO8UrrB4&t=8s**

1 kilogram beef
1 teaspoon (4 grams) turmeric powder
1 tablespoon (15 grams) chilli powder
2 tablespoons (30 grams) red chilli paste
3 teaspoons coriander powder
1 tablespoon (15 grams) ginger-garlic paste
2 medium onions, sliced
3 green chillies, slit

1 chicken stock cube
1 teaspoon (7 grams) salt
3 tablespoons (45 grams) oil
water, just enough to cover beef
2 tablespoons (30 grams) coconut oil
10 fresh curry leaves (about 5 grams)
1 kilogram Tapioca – cooked (Cook soft boil with 7g turmeric in water for 1kilo Tapioca)

METHOD

- Put beef and all ingredients except water, coconut oil,curry leaves and tapioca into a pressure cooker. Mix together.
- Pour in just enough water to cover the beef.
- Cook for 5 minutes with high pressure. Reduce the flame and cook for another 25 minutes on a low flame.
- When it is ready, open the pressure cooker lid and add the cooked tapioca, mixing in gently.
- Mix in the coconut oil and fresh whole curry leaves for an amazing flavour.
- Bring to a boil and serve hot.

Beef Short Rib Biriyani

Biryani is an exquisite rice dish originating from the Indian subcontinent. It consists of meat, rice, and spices. Beef short rib biryani is made up of beef ribs.

Video: https://www.youtube.com/watch?v=FNEA6S4LhY8&t=1s

For short rib

1 whole (400 grams) beef short rib
400 grams beef short rib, cut into small pieces
2 medium onions, sliced
2 tablespoons (30 grams) ginger garlic paste
5 tablespoons (75 grams) chopped tomato
1 teaspoon (7 grams) turmeric powder
1/4 teaspoon (3 grams) chilli powder (very hot)
4 tablespoons (60 grams) vegetable oil (all oil used can be veg oil)

1/2 cup (150 grams) thick yoghurt
1 teaspoon (7 grams) salt
3 teaspoons (21 grams) coriander powder
1/2 litre (500 mL) hot water
1 teaspoon (7 grams) garam masala
10 coriander shoots
8 coriander leaves, fresh
3 green chillies, sliced

To layer and finish biriyani

4 tablespoons (60 grams) oil
1 kilogram (1000 grams) beef short rib meat and sauce

1 kilogram (1000 grams) cooked basmati rice

METHOD

To pressure cook short rib

- In a pressure cooker, mix all the ingredients mentioned for the short rib, except the fresh coriander leaf and green chillies.
- Cover the pressure cooker and cook on high flame for 2 minutes.
- Bring it to down to low flame and cook for 40 minutes.
- When it is cooked, to finish the sauce, add the fresh coriander leaf and green chillies.

To layer and finish biriyani

- In a thick-bottom pan, pour 2 tablespoons oil.
- Pour 4 ladles of short rib sauce along with some meat pieces.
- Put a thin layer of cooked basmati rice on top of the sauce.
- For second layer, place the whole short rib, short rib pieces, and some sauce.

- Cover it with a layer of rice and pour remaining sauce and meat on top the rice.
- Finish by pouring 2 tablespoons of oil on top.
- Cover it with aluminium foil so no steam will escape. Then cover it with the lid.
- Cook on a high flame for a minute, then bring it to a low flame and cook for 6 minutes.
- Switch off the flame and let it rest for another 6 minutes before opening the lid.

For plating

- In a bowl, put the biriyani along with some short rib pieces.
- Place the whole short rib on top of the biriyani.
- (Optional) put some fresh mint, coriander leaf, and ginger juliennes on top for garnish.
- Serve hot.

Black Butter Chicken

Butter chicken is the most famous non-vegetarian dish of the Indian subcontinent. It is a curry of chicken in creamy tomato loaded with spices and butter. Black butter chicken is an interesting addition to classic butter chicken recipe. Charcoal powder is the star of the show.

Video: https://www.youtube.com/watch?v=rJokX_jDyso

For makhani sauce

2 cups (500 grams) butter chicken sauce (makhani sauce)
2 tablespoons (30 grams) butter
2 tablespoons (30 grams) double cream

a pinch (2 grams) fenugreek powder
1 teaspoon (7 grams) edible activated charcoal powder

For chicken tikka

3 skewers cooked chicken tikka
1 teaspoon (7 grams) olive oil

1 teaspoon (7 grams) water

For garnish

a pinch (1 gram) chat masala
a pinch (1 gram) fenugreek powder

1 teaspoon (7 grams) double cream
1/2 teaspoon (3 grams) brown onions

METHOD

To make makhana sauce

- In a pan, pour makhani sauce. Add butter, double cream, and fenugreek powder in to the sauce.
- Check the seasoning and add salt, sugar, and chilli powder if needed.
- Bring it to a low flame.
- In a small bowl, put charcoal powder and pour 2 ladles of makhani sauce.
- Mix it together and dilute the charcoal powder.
- Add it back to the makhani sauce in the pan and mix well until it turns to a nice black in colour.

To grill the chicken tikka

- Drizzle some olive oil and water on top the cooked chicken tikka.
- Place the chicken tikka on a hot grilling pan. Sear each side for 1 minute until it gets a nice colour.

For plating

- Place the grilled chicken tikka in a bowl and garnish it with chat masala, fenugreek powder, double cream, and brown onions.
- Pour the makhani sauce in a sauce bowl and pour it on top of chicken tikka while serving.

Buffalo Curry with Lemon Grass

Buffalo curry with lemon grass is a South Indian dish. This recipe is more on spicier side and it uses buffalo meat and is flavoured with lemon grass.

Video: https://www.youtube.com/watch?v=pR18rcYr7FA

INGREDIENTS

For marination

1 kg (1000 grams) buffalo meat, cut into 20-gram pieces
2 tablespoons (30 grams) ginger garlic paste
1 teaspoon (7 grams) turmeric powder
1 teaspoon (7 grams) pepper powder
3 teaspoons (21 grams) chilli powder
2 tablespoons (30 grams) coriander powder
1 teaspoon (7 grams) garam masala
1 tablespoon (15 grams) red chilli flakes

1 teaspoon (7 grams) salt
1 cube (20 grams) chicken stock cube
1 medium onion, sliced
4 green chillies, split
3/4 teaspoon (5 grams) curry leaf
2 tablespoons (30 grams) coconut oil
2 cups water
2 shoots lemongrass

For tempering (garnish)

1 tablespoon (15 grams) coconut oil
1 teaspoon (7 grams) garlic, julienned
3/4 teaspoon (5 grams) curry leaf

3/4 teaspoon (5 grams) lemongrass, chopped
3 green chillies, slit

METHOD

For marination

- In a pressure cooker, put the buffalo meat and add all the ingredients in the marination except lemongrass.
- Mix well and cook it at full pressure for 5 minutes.
- Reduce the flame and cook it on low pressure for 30 minutes.
- Once it is done, open the pressure cooker and add lemongrass.
- Cook it for few more minutes until the water is reduced to a semi-thick consistency and all the lemongrass flavour is infused.

For tempering (garnish)

- In a hot pan, pour coconut oil, add all mentioned ingredients in the tempering.
- Sauté for few minutes, sweating it until the nice aroma comes up.
- Pour it on top of the buffalo curry.

For plating

- In a nice bowl, pour the buffalo curry and put the tempering garnish on top of it.
- Serve.

Butter Chicken

Butter chicken is an amazing recipe that originated from the northern part of India. This is a world-famous dish where the gravy is prepared using tomato, butter, and cream.

Video: https://www.youtube.com/watch?v=DoWGDxb3ocM

INGREDIENTS

500 grams makhani sauce
500 grams tandoori chicken, cooked
7 tablespoons (100 grams) butter

1 teaspoon (7 grams) kasoori methi powder (fenugreek leaf)
salt, to taste
3 tablespoons (50 grams) double cream

For the garnish

2 coriander leaves
1 tablespoon (15 grams) crispy fried onions

1 tablespoon (15 grams) double cream

METHOD

- Heat makhani gravy and put cooked tandoori chicken into the gravy.
- Allow to boil and bring it to a low flame.
- Add butter, kasoori methi powder, salt, and double cream.
- Mix and allow to cook for 5 minutes.
- Place chicken in a bowl and pour makhani gravy over the chicken pieces.
- Garnish it with coriander leaf, crispy fried onions, and double cream.

Butter Chicken Biriyani

Butter chicken biriyani is an amazing combination of two famous dishes, butter chicken and biriyani.

Video: https://www.youtube.com/watch?v=6X3d_NcraPc

INGREDIENTS

4 tablespoons (60 grams) ghee, divided
1 kg butter chicken sauce with chicken pieces (500 g chicken, 500 g sauce)
1.5 kg cooked pilaf rice
4 tablespoons (60 grams) fried onions
8 Coriander leaves

mint leaf (optional)
6 green chillies, slit
3 tablespoons (45 grams) ginger, julienned
6 boiled eggs, Quartered
4 tablespoons water, to sprinkle

METHOD

- In a thick-bottom pot. Pour 2 tablespoons ghee.
- For first layer, pour butter chicken sauce with some chicken pieces.
- Arrange a layer of cooked pilaf rice on top.
- Put some fried onions, coriander leaf, slit green chilli, ginger, and boiled eggs on top of rice.
- Pour 1 tablespoon of ghee.
- Repeat the same to make second layer.
- Once all layers are done, sprinkle some water on top layer.
- Cover the pot with lid and keep it on a high flame for a minute.
- Cook it on a very low flame for another 15 minutes.
- Switch off the flame and leave it for another 10 minutes before opening the lid.
- Open the lid. Butter chicken biriyani is ready to serve.

For plating

- Serve it in a bowl and garnish it with coriander leaf, ginger, and fried onions.

Chicken Drumstick with Coconut

This is a unique and traditional recipe of South India. In this recipe, the chicken drumstick is cooked in a fried spicy, aromatic coconut mixture. This is a non-vegetarian side dish goes well with rice, porotta, and any type of bread.

Video: https://www.youtube.com/watch?v=cQymdL7CfrI&t=114s

1 kg (1000 grams) chicken drumsticks
2 tablespoons (30 grams) ginger garlic paste
½ teaspoon (3 grams) turmeric powder
2 teaspoons (14 grams) coriander powder
2 teaspoons (14 grams) chilli powder
1/4 teaspoons (3 grams) salt
1/4 teaspoons (3 grams) black pepper powder

1 cup (200 grams) coconut, freshly grated
2 tablespoons (30 grams) oil
Chicken skin from the drumsticks
3 dry red chillies
8 curry leaves
3 green chillies
1 teaspoon (7 grams) coconut oil

METHOD

To marinate chicken

- In a bowl, add chicken drumsticks, ginger garlic paste, turmeric powder, coriander powder, chilli powder, black pepper powder, and salt.
- Mix it altogether and keep it aside.

To make roasted coconut paste

- Put freshly grated coconut in a pan and roast it until it gets golden brown colour.
- Put the roasted coconut in a mixer jar, add water to just cover the roasted coconut, and grind it in to a fine paste.

To make chicken drumstick masala

- In a pan, pour oil. When the oil is hot, put chicken skin and sauté until it gets crispy. This is to extract the fat from the chicken skin and infuse the flavour into the oil. This method is called rendering.
- After doing this, you can discard the skin or keep it aside for garnish.
- Fry chicken drumstick in the same oil that is been rendered. Sear both sides for 2 minutes each.
- Break dry red chilli with your hand and put it on the chicken.
- Pour the roasted coconut paste, and mix it. Sauté until the chicken is cooked.
- If needed cover the pan with a lid and cook the chicken until the water gets reduced.
- Add curry leaf, slit green chilli, and coconut oil. Sauté for a minute.
- Plate it in a nice round plate and serve hot.

English Beef Steak and Chilli Pie

This wonderful recipe is inspired from an award-winning pie shop. Steak pie is a traditional English meal using slow-cooked beef and vegetables. Steak pie served with peas, mashed potatoes, and gravy is a classic combination.

Video: https://www.youtube.com/watch?v=LevoFs06StY&t=244s

INGREDIENTS

For beef pie mix

1 kg (1000 grams) beef, cut into cubes
2 tablespoons (30 grams) oil
1 teaspoon (7 grams) garlic, chopped
3 green chillies, chopped
1 medium onion, chopped
2 celery stems, chopped
1 tablespoon (15 grams) plain flour

1 tablespoon (15 grams) gravy granules
1 chicken stock cube, diluted in 100 ml hot water
1 teaspoon (7 grams) chilli flakes
300 mL water
3 coriander leaves
salt, to taste

For pie pastry

100 grams soft butter, cut into cubes
3/4 cup (200 gram) plain flour
1/2 teaspoon (4 grams) sugar

1/2 teaspoon (4 grams) salt
75 mL water

For garnish and to prepare pie

1 egg yolk, beaten with a touch of water   pastry strips from leftover pastry sheets
3/4 teaspoon (5 grams) roasted sesame seeds

METHOD

To make beef pie mix

- In a pressure cooker, pour some oil. When the oil is hot, add beef cubes.
- Sear for 3–4 minutes until beef becomes a nice brown colour.
- Add garlic and green chilli. Sauté for 2 minutes.
- Add onion and celery. Sauté for another 2 minutes.
- Add plain flour and mix well. This makes the sauce thicken and gives a shiny texture. Sauté for 2 minutes.
- Drop in gravy granules. Add chicken stock cube diluted in water. Allow to cook for another 2 minutes.
- To finish off, add chilli flakes, pour water, and mix well.
- Cook it by closing the pressure cooker lid. Cook for 2 minutes on high flame till the pressure is on.
- Then reduce to very slow flame and cook for 30 minutes.
- When it is done, open the lid and put in coriander leaves. Add salt to taste.
- If the pie mix is thin, cook it for few more minutes without closing the lid to thicken the gravy.
- The pie mix is ready. Keep it inside the fridge to cool it down.
- Line pie tin by applying butter. Once it is lined nicely, dust it with plain flour and keep it ready.
- Preheat the oven at 180 degrees C.

To make pie pastry

- In a mixing bowl, put butter, plain flour, sugar, and salt.
- Mix and crumb it with your hands.
- Add water and knead it in to a nice, soft pastry dough.
- Cling-film the dough and leave it inside the fridge for an hour.
- After an hour, take out the dough from the fridge and divide it into two halves.
- Place butter paper on a flat surface and dust it with plain flour.
- Place half of the dough on butter paper and slightly press it using your hands. Dust it with plain flour.

- Place another butter paper on top of the dough. Slightly press using hands and start rolling it using a rolling pin until it gets a nice circle shape.
- While rolling, make sure the pastry sheet is not too thin.
- Make sure the pastry sheet is bigger than the pie tin so that you get enough pastry to cover the side walls of the tin.
- Repeat the same process of rolling with second half of dough.
- Cut dough circles into the size of pie tin top to just cover the pie.

To arrange pie dish

- Place the pastry sheet in pie tin and slowly fold it into the pie tin.
- Using finger, slightly press the pastry to stick it into the edges and corners of the pie tin.
- Pour the pie mix in, fill the pie tin, and tap to make it even.
- Cover the pie mix with pastry sheet and apply egg wash to join the gaps over the edge.
- Towards the edge of the pie tin, run the knife around to take out excess pastry.
- Close the edge using fingers by slowly pressing it together.
- Make a hole at the middle of the pie for the steam to escape while cooking.
- Apply egg wash on top of the pie.
- You can arrange some of the leftover pastry strip on top of the pie to give nice texture and look. Also apply egg wash on top of the pastry strips to give nice colour.
- Sprinkle some roasted sesame seeds on top of the pie.
- Leave it in the fridge for half an hour so that dough will be rested and easy to bake.

To cook the pie

- Put the pie in the preheated oven and cook for 10 minutes.
- After 10 minutes, rotate and cook for another 15 minutes.
- Now the pie is ready. Apply some butter on top of the pie for the glaze.
- Before taking it out from the pie tin, let it cool down to room temperature. Then demould it by slowly lifting the pie from the pie tin.

Fish and Chips

Fish and chips is a hot dish that originated in England. This is made by frying fish in a batter and serving with chips. Fish and chips is the common take away food in United Kingdom. In my recipe, I am making beer batter to fry the fish.

Video: https://youtu.be/_pGb93Ew460

For batter

3 tablespoons (45 grams) plain flour
1 tablespoon (15 grams) rice flour
1 tablespoon (15 grams) corn flour
1/4 teaspoon (3 grams) baking powder

A pinch turmeric powder
1/2 teaspoon (4 grams) sugar
1/2 teaspoon (4 grams) salt
100 ml pale ale beer

For frying fish

5 pieces coley fish
2 tablespoons (30 grams) plain flour
1/4 teaspoon (2 grams) salt

1/4 teaspoon (2 grams) crushed black pepper
juice from 1/2 lemon
oil, to deep-fry

For plating

7 chips
2 tablespoons (30 grams) mushy peas
1 teaspoon (7 grams) tartar sauce

1 lime wedge
1 tablespoon (15 grams) applewood cheddar cheese

METHOD

To make the batter

- In a mixing bowl, put all the ingredients mentioned for making batter and mix well.
- To check the consistency of batter, put a finger in the batter and check whether it is coating the finger.
- Set it aside and let it rest for five minutes.

To fry the fish

- Lightly marinate the fish with some salt, crushed black pepper, and lemon juice.
- Dust the fish in plain flour by dipping the fish in the flour.
- Dip the fish in the batter and drop it in the hot oil.
- Deep-fry in hot oil at 170 degrees C for about 5 minutes.

For plating

- On a plate, arrange some chips.
- Put a tablespoon of mushy peas on top of the chips.
- Place the fish on top of the mushy peas.
- Put one more tablespoon of mushy peas on top of the fish and place the lime wedge.
- Keep tartar sauce on the side of the plate.
- Garnish the fish with some grated applewood cheddar cheese and serve hot.

Grilled Lamb Ribs Masala

This is a beautiful recipe where lamb ribs are marinated using Indian spices and served with an Indian spice–infused chutney or sauce.

Videos

Grilled Lamb Ribs: https://www.youtube.com/watch?v=LFBgQpaqOP0

Saag Aloo: https://www.youtube.com/watch?v=0Xbz0B40jng

INGREDIENTS

For Marination

lamb breast with the bone

1 teaspoon (7 grams) ginger garlic paste
1/4 teaspoon (3 grams) turmeric powder
1/4 teaspoon (3 grams) black pepper powder

1/4 teaspoon (3 grams) salt
1 teaspoon (7 grams) lemon juice
1 tablespoon (15 grams) olive oil

For sauce (salsa chutney)

2 garlic cloves
1 1/2 teaspoons (10 grams) ginger, fresh
1 Holland red chilli
4 coriander leaves, fresh

1 tablespoon (15 grams) lemon juice
A pinch (2 grams) salt
2 tablespoons (30 grams) hot olive oil

- Marinate the lamb using the ingredients mentioned in the marination.
- Marinate the lamb for at least an hour.
- Using a mortar and pestle, crush all the ingredients mentioned in the sauce except hot olive oil.
- Once it is crushed, pour the hot olive oil on top of the crushed ingredients and mix well. Set aside
- In a hot open grilling pan, place the lamb by keeping the fat side on the grill.
- Cook for 2 minutes on a medium flame.
- When the fat is rendered or melted, turn the side. Cook this side for 3–4 minutes because this is the bone side.
- The grilled lamb ribs are ready. Serve hot with saag aloo.
- Serve a small bowl of salsa chutney on the side.

Nandos Spicy Rice

This is an excellent rice recipe and one-pot rice dish. It is a simple recipe to make with everyday cupboard spices.

Video: https://www.youtube.com/watch?v=gzkgDADSMg0&t=11s

For spice mix

2 teaspoon (14 grams) garlic powder
4 teaspoons (28 grams) dry onion powder
1 teaspoon (7 grams) turmeric powder
½ teaspoon (3 grams) Chilli powder

1 teaspoon (7 grams) smoked paprika powder
1 teaspoon (7 grams) coriander powder
1 teaspoon (7 grams) cumin powder
1 teaspoon (7 grams) dry coriander leaves

For cooking rice

2 cups (500 grams) long grain rice
5 tablespoons (75 grams) olive oil
2 bell peppers (green and red), chopped
1 Holland red chilli, diced
5 teaspoons (32 grams) spice mix

1 vegetable stock cube
2 teaspoons (14 grams) salt
1/2 cup (100 grams) passata sauce
3/4 cup (850 grams) water
2 tablespoons (30 grams) lemon juice

METHOD

To make spice mix

- Put all the ingredients in the spice mix section in a small bowl and mix.

For cooking rice

- In a pot, pour olive oil. When the oil is hot, put chopped bell peppers and Holland red chilli. Sauté for 2 minutes.
- Add spice mix and sauté for 1 minute.
- Add vegetable stock cube and sauté for another minute.
- Add salt and passata sauce, and sauté for 1 minute.
- Add in long grain rice and mix for 1 minute.
- Add water. When the water starts boiling, add lemon juice.
- Once the water is reduced and absorbed, cover the pot with aluminium foil and an airtight lid.
- Cook it on a low flame for 6 minutes, then switch it off and rest it for another 6 minutes before opening the lid.
- Serve it in a side bowl.

Peri Peri Chicken

This amazing recipe is a replication of Nandos peri peri chicken. Here, we are using the poaching method to cook the chicken leg.

Video: https://www.youtube.com/watch?v=PBC5WnNMQrc&t=1s

INGREDIENTS

To poach chicken leg

3 chicken legs (curing in salt for 30 minutes optional)
1 litre water

2 chicken stock cubes
1/4 teaspoon (3 grams) chilli flakes
2 spring onions

For marinade

1/4 teaspoon (3 grams) chilli flakes
1 tablespoon (15 grams) olive oil

2 tablespoons (30 grams) soya sauce

For plating

2 grilled spring onions

1 tablespoon (15 grams) nandos peri peri sauce

METHOD

To poach chicken leg

- Score chicken leg using knife and set aside.
- In a pan, pour water and allow it to boil.
- Add chicken stock cubes and chilli flakes.
- Put chicken leg in the boiling water and reduce the flame to very low.
- Allow to cook the chicken on a low flame (98 degrees C) for 15 minutes without covering the pan.
- Put spring onion in to the pan along with the chicken and switch off the flame.
- Take out the spring onion from the water after 2 minutes and set it aside.
- Allow chicken to cool down in the pan in stock water. By doing this, the chicken will get more juicy and flavourful.

To grill chicken

- Make marinade with chilli flakes, olive oil, and soya sauce.
- Apply marinade to cooked chicken and spring onions.

- Preheat the grilling pan. When the pan is hot, grill chicken on skin side first for 2 minutes until the chicken gets a nice grill colour.
- Repeat on other side of the chicken.
- Before removing chicken from the pan, spread nandos peri peri sauce on top of the chicken.
- Remove chicken from the grill pan and get ready to plate.
- Put spring onion into the pan to grill. Leave it for 40 seconds and then remove. Set aside for garnish.

For plating

- Place chicken on a serving plate and put grilled spring onions on top.
- Pour some nandos peri peri sauce on the side and serve.

Steam Chicken

This is the easiest and healthiest chicken recipe. It is best served with crushed ginger and spring onion chutney. Steam chicken best retains the flavour, moisture, and tenderness of the chicken and thus makes chicken recipes more flavoursome.

Video: https://www.youtube.com/watch?v=MaNF4egPyXs&t=5s

INGREDIENTS

3 chicken quarters with skin on
1/2 juice of a lime

To steam chicken

2 tablespoons (30 grams) sliced onion
2 tablespoons (30 grams) sliced carrot

For plating

3 tablespoons (50 grams) steamed sliced onion,
carrot, and cabbage

1/4 teaspoon (3 grams) salt
1/4 teaspoon (2 grams) black pepper, crushed

2 tablespoons (30 grams) sliced cabbage

3 tablespoons (50 grams) ginger and spring onion
chutney

METHOD

- Marinate the chicken quarters with lime juice, salt, and pepper. Leave it to rest for 5 minutes.
- In a steamer, put sliced onion, carrot, and cabbage.
- Arrange chicken on top of sliced veggies without overlapping.
- Cover and steam for 25 minutes on medium heat.
- Serve hot along with ginger and spring onion chutney and steamed veggies.

Steamed Curried Mussels with Coconut and Leeks

This fantastic mussel recipe is easy to cook. I used Indian flavours to make these deliciously steamed and curried mussels.

Video: https://www.youtube.com/watch?v=PXdDqRlBpnE&t=1s

INGREDIENTS

1 kg (1000 grams) mussels (with shell)
2 tablespoons (30 grams) coconut oil
1/4 teaspoon (3 grams) asafoetida (hing)
1/2 tablespoon (5 grams) mustard seeds
1 tablespoon (15 grams) ginger, julienned
1 tablespoon (15 grams) garlic, julienned
2 green chillies, finely sliced
1 leek stem, sliced

1 medium onion, chopped
1/2 teaspoon (4 grams) turmeric powder
salt, to taste
2 tablespoons (30 grams) coconut, grated
6 baby plum tomatoes, cut in half
2 green chillies, slit
6 curry leaves

METHOD

To clean mussels

- Put mussels in a bowl under fresh running water. When the mussels are dropped into the water, they will open up to get more oxygen.
- Leave in the water for at least 6 hours.
- In this way, whatever dirt collected inside the mussel shell will go out and wash away.
- After 6 hours, take out the dead mussels that are floating and throw them away.
- Clean and change water at least 3 times.
- Take mussels one by one and take out the fibre part or sandy part from the mussels.

To cook mussels

- Heat a thick-bottom pan and pour in coconut oil.
- When the oil is hot, add asafoetida and mustard seeds. Allow them to crack.
- Add ginger and garlic. Sauté till light brown in colour.
- Add in finely sliced green chilli, leeks, chopped onions, and turmeric powder. Sauté for 2 minutes.
- Add mussels and mix. Cover the pot with a lid and cook for 5 minutes.
- After 5 minutes, open the lid and check the seasoning. At this stage, add salt if needed.
- Add the grated coconut, baby plum tomatoes, green chilli, and curry leaf. Mix.
- The mussels are hot and ready to serve.

Tandoori Chicken Biriyani

Tandoori chicken biriyani is a popular Indian rice-based dish consisting of roasted tandoori chicken. It is most commonly prepared using basmati rice. This biriyani is made with spices and chicken. Here, chicken is marinated with tandoori masala and yoghurt.

Video: https://www.youtube.com/watch?v=PRQgvR6Q-2o&t=1s

2 kg (2000 grams) tangdi chicken curry
2 kg (2000 grams) cooked pilaf rice
1 whole tandoori chicken, cooked

8 fresh mint leaves
8 fresh coriander leaves
2 tablespoons (30 grams) ghee

METHOD

For layering the biriyani

- In a big pot, pour some tangdi chicken curry sauce.
- Layer some cooked pilaf rice on top of the gravy. This is the first layer of rice.
- Arrange some chicken drumsticks from the tangdi chicken curry on top of the rice. Make sure you have enough pieces for two layers.
- Pour some curry sauce; this gives the steam for the biriyani to get properly dum.
- Break fresh mint leaves and coriander leaves and put it on top.
- Repeat the second layer.
- On top of the second layer, put some cooked rice and pour some tangdi chicken curry sauce.
- To finish, add ghee on top, cover the pot, and keep it on a high heat for 2 minutes.
- Bring it down to a very low heat for 15 minutes.
- When it's done, open the lid and slowly mix the biriyani.

For plating

- In a big serving dish, put some biriyani rice along with the chicken drumsticks.
- Place the whole tandoori chicken on top of the biriyani.
- Garnish with some fresh coriander leaf and serve.

Tangdi Chicken Curry

This is a special chicken curry found in southern part of India, in Hyderabad. This chicken curry is made with Indian spices mixed with yoghurt. Chicken drumsticks are the best chicken part to do tangdi, or you can use any part of the chicken with a bone. I use this recipe as the base for my chicken curry .

Video: https://youtu.be/YOB7kORJ6ng

2 tablespoons (30 grams) oil
1 teaspoon (7 grams) whole spices
2 medium onions, sliced
3 tablespoons (45 grams) ginger garlic paste
1/2 teaspoon (4 grams) turmeric powder
3 teaspoons (21 grams) chilli powder
3 teaspoon (21 grams) coriander powder
4 tablespoons (60 grams) Greek yoghurt

1/4 teaspoon (3 grams) garam masala
1/4 teaspoon (3 grams) cardamom powder
1 teaspoon (7 grams) salt
10 chicken drumsticks (1.5 kg)
500 mL hot water
4 fresh mint leaves
4 fresh coriander leaves

METHOD

- In a hot pot, pour oil. Put in whole spices and allow it to pop.
- Add sliced onions and sauté for 3 minutes.
- Now add ginger garlic paste and sauté for 2 minutes.
- Add in turmeric powder, chilli powder, and coriander powder. Sauté for 1 minute.
- Put in Greek yoghurt, garam masala, cardamom powder, and salt. Mix.
- Put in chicken drumsticks, sauté, and mix well for 3 minutes until the chicken leaves water.
- Pour in hot water and cook it for 20 minutes on a slow flame, covering the pot with a lid.
- To finish the curry, put fresh mint leaves and coriander leaves into the curry.
- The tangdi chicken curry is ready to serve.

Turkey leg drumstick Tandoori

Tandoori turkey legs Drumstick are an amazing dish. Turkey drumsticks are roasted after marinating in a tangy, spicy tandoori sauce. Tandoori turkey legs have all the flavour from an Indian tandoori recipe, but using turkey drumsticks gives it a more earthy, savoury result over chicken.

Video: https://www.youtube.com/watch?v=m-x8LYqi-Hc

INGREDIENTS

1 leg (750 grams) turkey leg, skin removed

For first marination

2 tablespoons (30 grams) ginger garlic paste
2 teaspoons (14 grams) chilli powder
1/2 teaspoon (4 grams) turmeric powder

1/2 teaspoon (4 grams) salt
1 tablespoon (15 grams) lemon juice

For second marination

4 tablespoon (60 grams) yoghurt
1 tablespoon (15 grams) corn flour
1 teaspoon (7 grams) chilli powder
1/4 teaspoon (3 grams) black pepper powder

1/2 teaspoon (4 grams) salt
1/2 teaspoon (4 grams) garam masala powder
1/4 teaspoon (2 grams) cardamom powder
1 tablespoon (15 grams) oil (plain)

METHOD

- Score the turkey drumstick. Make an incision to get the marinade inside and to cook faster.
- Apply the first marinate using all the ingredients mentioned in the first marination.
- Keep it in the fridge overnight for the best results.
- Apply the second marinade and keep it for at least an hour.
- Preheat the oven to 220 degrees C and cook for 10 minutes.
- Apply oil or butter on top of the meat.
- Reduce the heat to 170 degrees C and cook for another 20 minutes.
- Sprinkle some chat masala and lemon juice.
- Serve hot.

Whole Fried Chicken

This fried chicken recipe is marinated in Indian spices. Cut the whole chicken in a spatchcock style. Marinate whole cut chicken for frying and rest for an hour before frying. Fried whole chicken can be used in restaurants for sharing portions.

Video: https://www.youtube.com/watch?v=aSxSRM-ImX0

INGREDIENTS

1 whole chicken

oil, to deep-fry

For crushed spices masala

2 whole red chillies
1 teaspoon (7 grams) black pepper whole
1 tablespoon (15 grams) ginger, fresh
6 garlic cloves

4 green chillies
1 teaspoon (7 grams) cloves
1 teaspoon (7 grams) fennel
2 tablespoons (30 grams) lime juice

For marinating chicken

4 tablespoons (60 grams) crushed spices masala
1/4 teaspoon (3 grams) turmeric powder
1 teaspoon (7 grams) Kashmiri chilli powder

1 tablespoon (15 grams) lime juice
1/2 teaspoon (5 grams) salt
1 tablespoon (15 grams) rice flour

For plating

wooden board
1 medium onion, thinly sliced
1 green chilli, slit

To make crushed spices masala

- Put all the ingredients mentioned in crushed spices masala in a mortar and finely crush it using a pestle.

To marinate chicken

- Apply crushed spice masala on chicken, carefully applying it through every cut.
- Set aside and let it rest for at least half an hour.
- After half an hour, mix turmeric powder, chilli powder, lime juice, and salt. Apply and massage nicely on chicken.
- Let it rest for another 5 minutes.
- Before frying, add rice flour and massage. This gives the nice crust.

To fry chicken

- In a hot frying pan, pour oil.
- When the oil is hot (170 degrees C), carefully put the marinated chicken into the oil.
- After 7 minutes, turn to the other side and fry for another 7 minutes.
- Fry at least 15 minutes altogether.
- When it is done, carefully lift the chicken from the oil and place it on a towel to drain the excess oil.

For plating

- On the wooden board, place the fried chicken.
- Serve it with thinly sliced onions. Before serving sliced onions, wash it in ice cold water to get rid of the pungency and the smell.
- Keep slit green chilli on top of the onion slices.

Whole Tandoori Chicken

Tandoori chicken is the most familiar Indian food around the world. This tandoori chicken is cooked without a tandoori oven. Here, the whole chicken is marinated in tandoori marinade and cooked inside a conventional oven.

Video: https://www.youtube.com/watch?v=5BlztaMXkhQ&t=22s

INGREDIENTS

1 whole chicken

For first marination

2 tablespoons (30 grams) ginger garlic paste
2 teaspoons (14 grams) chilli powder
1/2 teaspoon (4 grams) turmeric powder

1/2 teaspoon (4 grams) salt
1 tablespoon (15 grams) lemon juice

For second marination

4 tablespoons (60 grams) yoghurt
1 tablespoon (15 grams) corn flour
1 teaspoon (7 grams) chilli powder
1/4 teaspoon (3 grams) black pepper powder

1/2 teaspoon (4 grams) salt
1/2 teaspoon (4 grams) garam masala powder
1/4 teaspoon (2 grams) cardamom powder
1 tablespoon (15 grams) oil (plain)

METHOD

To prepare the chicken

- Remove the winglets from both sides.
- Make a slit at the back of the chicken using a knife.
- Run your fingers in between the skin and body. Try to remove the skin by running your finger under the chicken skin, and pull the skin out from the leg.
- Try not to break the skin so you will not lose grip.
- Do the same on the breast side of the chicken and remove the skin through the wings.
- For excess skin on the wings, take it off using a knife.
- If needed, you can remove the extra fat on the chicken.
- Run the knife lengthways on the chicken breast to score the breast. Doing this makes it cook faster, and the marinade goes inside the chicken.
- Repeat the same method on other chicken breast.
- Scrape the wing bone and remove it.
- Score the chicken legs using a knife.

For first marination

- In a bowl, put all the ingredients mentioned in the first marinade. Mix well and make it into a nice paste.
- Apply this marinade to the chicken. If needed, you can keep it in the fridge overnight, or you can cook straight away.

For second marination

- In a bowl, put all the ingredients mentioned in the second marination. Mix well and make it into a paste without any lumps.
- Add in the oil and mix well. This gives a nice shine to the marinade.
- Apply the second marinade on the chicken and leave to rest for at least half an hour before cooking.

For cooking tandoori chicken

- If it is a gas-fired conventional oven, preheat the oven to 250 degrees C.
- Place the marinated chicken in the oven grill.
- Cook it for 10 minutes.
- Bring the heat down to 180 degrees C and cook it for another 20 minutes.
- The chicken is fully cooked and ready to serve.

Wood Pigeon Green Chutney Biriyani

Biryani is a fragrant and spiced dish that complements well with wood pigeon. This recipe calls for wood pigeon and green chutney, which adds flavour to the already flavoursome food.

Video: https://www.youtube.com/watch?v=bjVGBiCXLEk

INGREDIENTS

For wood pigeon marination

3 tablespoons (50 grams) ginger
3 tablespoons (50 grams) garlic
3 teaspoons (21 grams) whole black pepper, crushed

3 teaspoons (21 grams) whole cloves
3 teaspoons (21 grams) lemon juice
1 teaspoon (7 grams) salt

Cooked rice

To make green chutney

10 grams mint leaf 1
40 grams coriander leaf
4 green chillies
3 garlic cloves

1 teaspoon (7 grams) whole black pepper
1 teaspoon (7 grams) fennel seeds
20g roasted peanuts

For cooking pigeon

1 wood pigeon, marinated
1/2 cup (125 grams) ghee (clarified butter)
1 teaspoon (7 grams) turmeric powder
3 teaspoons (21 grams) coriander powder
1/4 teaspoon (3 grams) salt

1 teaspoon (7 grams) black pepper powder
1 cup (300 grams) thick Greek yoghurt, beaten
1/2 cup (100 grams) fried onions
3 cups hot water

To cook rice

1 kg (1000 grams) basmati rice (sella), soaked in water for 30 minutes and drained
1 ladle (30 grams) ghee (clarified butter)
2 tablespoons (30 grams) whole spice
4 tablespoons (60 grams) sliced onions
1 teaspoon (7 grams) powdered cardamom

1 teaspoon (7 grams) powdered mace
juice from 1 medium lemon
1 teaspoon (7 grams) salt
1.7 litres (1700 grams) water (boiled)
4 mint leaves
4 coriander leaves

To finish biriyani

1 cup (300 mL) double cream
green chutney

3 tablespoons (50 grams) fried onions

6 boiled eggs, cut in half

METHOD

- Make a paste using all the ingredients mentioned in the marination.
- Apply marination paste to wood pigeon and set it aside.
- Put all the ingredients mentioned in the green chutney in a mixer jar and grind it into a smooth paste.
- Cook the rice and keep it ready.

To cook pigeon

- In a thick-bottom pot, pour the ghee.
- When the ghee is hot, add marinated wood pigeon one by one to sear.
- Sauté and cook for at least 2 minutes.
- Add turmeric powder, coriander powder, salt, and black pepper powder and sauté for 3 minutes.
- Add yoghurt and sauté gently for 1 minute.
- Add fried onions, mix, and pour in hot water.
- Cover and cook for two hours on a low flame.

To finish biriyani

- Take out all the wood pigeon pieces from the cooking pot.
- Add double cream to the sauce in the pot and cook until the sauce is reduced.
- Add green chutney paste, mix it, and cook it for 1 minute.
- Take out half the amount of sauce and set it aside.
- Put a few pieces of cooked pigeons back into the pot.
- Add a layer of cooked rice on top of the pigeon.
- Put another layer of cooked pigeon on top of the cooked rice.
- Pour in some of the sauce that you kept aside.

- Layer some boiled egg and fried onions.
- Put another layer of rice, pour sauce, and layer boiled eggs and fried onions.
- Cover the pot with aluminium foil so the steam will not escape.
- Cover with lid and cook for 15 minutes on a low flame.
- Serve hot.

Dessert

Banana Pudding

Banana pudding is a dessert commonly associated with the cuisine of the South American. My recipe is inspired by one of Magnolia Bakery's best-selling dishes. Banana pudding consists of layers of sweet vanilla-flavoured custard, Swiss roll, and banana, topped with whipped cream. This dessert is a good compliment for Indian dishes.

Video: **https://www.youtube.com/watch?v=wXEQ5ilXfu8&t=1s**

INGREDIENTS

For whipped cream
7 tablespoons (100 grams) whipped cream powder

For custard

3 tablespoons (45 grams) sugar
1 tablespoon (15 grams) corn flour
3 egg yolks

3 ripe bananas, soaked in milk

1 tablespoon (15 grams) vanilla essence
1/2 cup (125 grams) milk
1 cup (200 grams) Swiss roll, cut into small pieces

METHOD

To make whipped cream

- Put whipped cream powder in a bowl.
- Remove the banana from the milk and set aside. Add the banana-infused milk to the whipped cream powder.
- Mix using a hand blender, slowly at first, then beating until it foams.
- The whipped cream has reached the right consistency when you can gently tilt the bowl upside down without the cream falling out.

To make custard

- Put all the custard ingredients into a pan.
- Using a whisk, mix it slowly, making sure there are no lumps.
- Set the pan on a low fire and cook, stirring continuously so the mixture won't stick on the bottom of the pan.
- Stir until it becomes thick, then set aside to cool to room temperature.

To assemble pudding

- Pour the cooled custard into a large bowl. Add 2 tablespoons of the whipped cream and fold to mix in.
- Add the remaining whipped cream to the custard. Gently fold the whipped cream into the custard until it becomes fluffy. Try to retain the volume of air. Stirring too vigorously will cause the custard to liquify.

- Add the soaked banana and fold in.
- Add the pieces of Swiss roll, reserving crumbs for garnish later to top the pudding. Slowly fold to incorporate.
- Transfer to a larger bowl and keep in the fridge to set for at least 6 hours.

For plating

- For each serving, spoon the banana pudding into a small deep bowl.
- Sprinkle leftover Swiss roll crumbs on top.
- Garnish with mixed berries and grated chocolate.
- Serve immediately.

Cream Cheese Kulfi

Cream cheese kulfi is a different kulfi recipe which uses cream cheese for added creaminess. Traditionally, kulfi is made with malai, but this kulfi has hints of cream cheese, and a more English touch is added by topping with crunchy pastry sheets and grated chocolate.

Video: https://www.youtube.com/watch?v=OyUWUWWAjSg

2 tablespoons (30 grams) cream cheese
3 tablespoons (45 grams) condensed milk

1 teaspoon (7 grams) cardamom sugar

For crispy spring roll sheet

1 spring roll sheet, cut into shreds

oil, to fry

For garnish

1/4 teaspoon (3 grams) cardamom sugar

1 teaspoon (7 grams) dark chocolate, grated

METHOD

- In a mixing bowl, put cream cheese, condensed milk, and cardamom sugar.
- Using whisk, mix well until it gets a nice, shiny texture.
- Pour the mixture into an ice cream mould or into any container and put it in the freezer to set.

For crispy spring roll sheet

- Cut the spring roll sheet into thin shreds.
- Pour oil in a hot pan and deep-fry the shredded spring roll sheet.
- Set it aside on a towel to drain out the excess oil.

For plating

- Demould the kulfi by dipping the container or ice cream mould in hot water.
- Cut the kulfi into wedges.
- Place a wedge in a bowl and put the fried spring roll sheet on top the kufi.
- Dust cardamom sugar and grate the dark chocolate on top of the kulfi.
- Serve.

Fluffy Coconut Pancakes

One of the most sought-after breakfast dishes is pancakes. Fluffy coconut pancakes are different than classic pancakes because they use coconut milk powder and hot chocolate mix. What makes this dish unique is the blueberry cardamom compote, which adds to the flavour.

Video: https://www.youtube.com/watch?v=0jxDbyG3oaI

INGREDIENTS

For hot chocolate sauce

2 tablespoons (30 grams) hot chocolate mix
2 tablespoons (30 grams) chocolate hazelnut spread (Nutella)

5 tablespoons (75 grams) hot milk

For blueberry cardamom compote

1 cup (200 grams) blueberries
1/2 lemon or lime juice
1/2 grated lime zest

1/4 teaspoon (3 grams) cardamom powder
2 tablespoons (30 grams) golden syrup

For pancake mix

1 egg
1/4 teaspoon (3 grams) salt
2 tablespoons (30 grams) brown sugar
4 tablespoons (60 grams) coconut milk powder
2 tablespoons (30 grams) corn flour

2 cups (400 grams) cold milk
2 cups (500 grams) self-raising or plain flour
1/4 teaspoon (2 grams) baking powder
3 tablespoons (50 grams) melted butter

For assembling pancake stack

3 pancake
3 tablespoons (45 grams) blueberry compote
1 whole banana, sliced
3 tablespoons (45 grams) chocolate sauce

3 tablespoons (45 grams) vanilla fresh cream
1/4 teaspoon (3 grams) grated lime zest
1 teaspoon (7 grams) Coco Pops

METHOD

To make chocolate sauce

- In a small mixing bowl put hot chocolate mix, Nutella and hot milk.
- Mix it altogether, make it in to a smooth paste and keep it aside.

To make blueberry cardamom compote

- In a hot pan, put blueberry, lemon juice, lime zest, cardamom powder, and golden syrup.
- Allow the berries to cook for at least 5 minutes until the water from the blueberries reduces.
- Now the compote is nicely cooked and thickened.
- Set it aside and let it cool down.

To make pancake mix

- In a mixing bowl, put egg, salt, and sugar. Beat using a whisk until it is light and airy.
- Add coconut milk powder and mix it nicely.
- Add corn flour and mix it.
- Add 100 grams of milk and mix it so there are no lumps.
- Add 1 cup of self-rising flour and mix it into a smooth texture.
- Add 300 grams milk and 1 more cup of self-rising flour. Mix well until the batter is bit airy and fluffy.
- Add baking powder and mix well. Add melted butter and mix well.

To cook pancakes

- In a preheated non-stick pan, apply butter and spoon in the pancake mix.
- Cover the pan with a lid and cook it for two minutes.

- After 2 minutes, flip the pancake and apply some melted butter.
- Cover the pan with a lid and cook for another 2 minutes.

For assembling the pancake stack

- On a plate, place one pancake and put blueberry compote on top of the pancake.
- Arrange sliced banana on top of blueberry compote and drizzle some chocolate sauce.
- Put another layer of pancake and repeat the process.
- Make three layers of pancake by repeating the process.
- Top it with some vanilla fresh cream.
- Grate some lime zest and put Coco Pops on top of the vanilla cream.
- While serving pancake on the table, pour chocolate sauce on top.

Foraged Wild Raspberry and Rice Payasam Souffle

This French baked egg dish has an Indian touch to it. Freshness from wild raspberries and rice payasam is what makes this dish so flavourful.

Video: https://www.youtube.com/watch?v=_a1xieLPSuQ

INGREDIENTS

For payasam base

1 cup wild raspberries
3 tablespoons rice flour
3/4 cup milk
1 tablespoon butter

2 tablespoons brown sugar
1 tablespoon cardamom sugar
1/4 teaspoon salt

For souffle meringue:

2 tablespoons brown sugar, powdered

2 egg whites

For souffle mould

1 table spoon soft butter

2 tablespoon brown sugar

METHOD

For payasam base

- In a pan, pour milk. Dissolve rice flour while milk is cold.
- Cook over a low heat while mixing well without any lumps, until the mixture is white and thick.
- Add raspberries and cook until they are smashed and mixed well with the white mixture.
- Finish with cardamom sugar, butter, and salt.
- Mix well and set it aside to cool down.

For souffle meringue

- Beat the egg whites with the electric whisk by adding powdered brown sugar in intervals.
- Check the consistency of the meringue. Whisk until it gets the soft peak consistency.
- Do the meringue test by holding the bowl upside down. If it is not falling off, it is a good meringue.

For souffle

- Preheat the oven to 180 degrees C for 10 minutes.
- Line the souffle mould with butter and coat it with brown sugar.
- In a bowl, mix two tablespoons of meringue and 3 tablespoons of payasam base together to get a smooth paste.
- Add the paste to the remaining souffle meringue. Fold it nicely using a silicon spatula.
- Put the souffle mix into the mould to the top. Run your finger around the tip of the souffle mould and wipe off the sides.
- Bake in the oven for 10 minutes.
- Serve. Garnish with raspberry, cardamom sugar, and raspberry flower.

Waffles

This is an incredible, home-made bubble waffle made in a waffle maker. This waffle recipe is easy and makes delicious waffles. I serve it with mixed berries, cake cubes, maple syrup, ice cream, grated chocolate, and some marshmallows.

Video: https://www.youtube.com/watch?v=P-FTbajgYc4&t=17s

INGREDIENTS

For waffle

10 tablespoons (150 grams) plain flour	2 tablespoons (30 grams) butter, clarified
3 tablespoons (50 grams) corn flour	1/2 teaspoon (4 grams) vinegar
1 teaspoon (7 grams) baking powder	2 eggs
1/4 teaspoon (3 grams) baking soda	1/2 cup (150 mL) milk
1/4 teaspoon (3 grams) salt	1/4 teaspoon (3 grams) vanilla essence
1 1/2 teaspoons (10 grams) brown sugar	

For plating

1 tablespoon (15 grams) mixed berries	1 teaspoon (7 grams) maple syrup
1 tablespoon (15 grams) cake cubes	1/4 teaspoon (3 grams) grated chocolate
1 scoop ice cream	1 tablespoon (15 grams) marshmallow

METHOD

- In a bowl, put plain flour, corn flour, baking powder, baking soda, salt, and brown sugar. Mix and set aside.
- In another bowl, pour clarified butter, vinegar, eggs, milk, and vanilla essence. Using a beater mix it altogether.

- Pour the flour mix into the butter mixture bowl.
- Using the beater, mix it and make it into a batter.
- Preheat the waffle maker. Apply clarified butter in waffle maker to get nice colour and caramelised flavour to the waffle.
- Put the waffle batter in a squeezy bottle and squeeze the batter into the waffle maker. Make sure to fill in all the bubbles
- Close the waffle maker and cook for 3 minutes.
- When it is ready, take it out and make it into a cone shape.
- Serve it with all the ingredients mentioned for plating.

Beverage

Cold-Brew Coffee

This is delicious and refreshing cold-brew coffee made from fresh, 100% Colombian coffee powder. This coffee is served over ice with milk.

Video: https://www.youtube.com/watch?v=9VTjPFfN4rk

glass jar that can hold 500 grams
3 cups cold water
2 tablespoons (30 grams) Colombian coffee powder

4 ice cubes
30 mL milk

METHOD

- In the glass jar, pour 3 cups of cold water and add coffee powder into the water.
- Mix it, close the glass jar tightly, and keep it in the fridge for 24 hours.
- After 24 hours, pass the coffee through a fine sieve to get a very clear coffee brew.
- Put ice cubes in a glass and pour the coffee on top.
- Add milk and serve.

Karak Tea Masala Chai

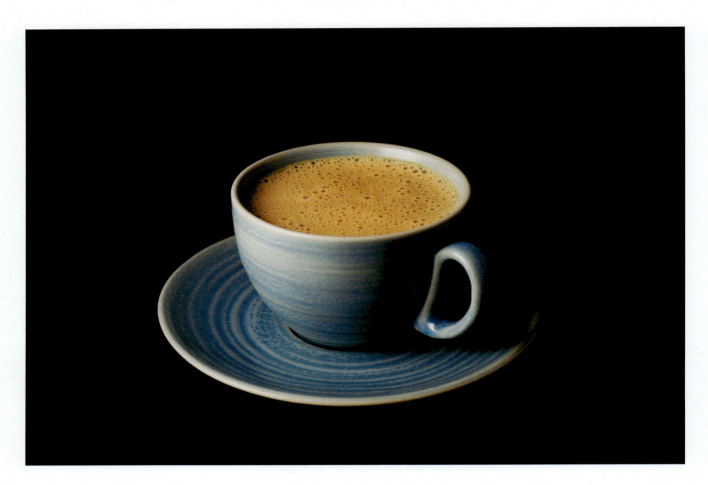

This is the most famous tea beverage of India because it conforms to the taste palette of every Indian. In this beverage, black tea is brewed with Indian spices, milk, and sugar.

Video: https://www.youtube.com/watch?v=0Pe7S5GUVmo&t=7s

1 tablespoon (15 grams) cardamom pods (15 pods)

1 tablespoon (20 grams) fresh ginger

4 cups milk

4 tablespoons (60 grams) loose tea leaves

A pinch (1 gram) salt

4 teaspoons (28 grams) sugar

METHOD

- To make a masala mix, put cardamom pods and ginger in a mortar and crush with a pestle.
- In a pot, pour milk. Put masala mix and tea leaves into the milk and mix well.
- Boil the milk. Once it starts boiling, add salt and sugar and mix well.
- Boil it for 2 more minutes.
- Strain the tea and mix the tea by pouring it from the top using a cup.
- Pour it into a teacup and serve it hot.

Printed in the United States
by Baker & Taylor Publisher Services